W9-BEQ-104

Pets

Never Dance with a Tree Frog

by Anita Higman

Perfection Learning®

To my wondrous kids, Scott and Hillary,
who keep me ever looking at life through the eyes of imagination.

About the Author

Anita Higman is the published author of numerous articles and stories as well as a book of one-act plays and a gift book of poetry.

She was the co-host of a radio talk show called *Open Line* and producer of a television show for children called *The Kids Story House.*

Mrs. Higman lives in Texas with her husband, two children, and their pet salamander named Chompers. Mrs. Higman loves reading, hiking, and eating anything made out of chocolate. She and her family are building a nature trail through the woods in western Oklahoma, where Mrs. Higman grew up.

Acknowledgments

My deep gratitude goes to Sheridan L. Duncan, D.V.M., for his informative and thoughtful answers to a myriad questions about pets.

Also, a generous thank-you goes to these lovely people who supplied me with fun and interesting information about pets.

Suzanne Locker (owner of a boarding house for pets)

Angel Tenant (manager of a pet-care facility)

Christine Lewis-Lyman (rancher and breeder)

At Perfection Learning Corporation, I am very grateful to my editors, Jody Cosson and Sue Thies, for their helpful and patient attitudes, which made writing for them a real joy.

I would also like to express my appreciation to Kimberly, Brandon, Edwin, and Peter for their wonderful cat stories. And Patti, Scott, Hillary, Hannah, and Andrea for their help and support.

PLEASE NOTE:

Any statements or opinions in this book should not be considered a substitute for acquiring your own individualized, professional pet-care advice.

Also, this book is meant to provide a general overview of pet care rather than detailed instructions. Please read a more specific care guide for the type of pet you intend to buy.

Text © 1997 by Perfection Learning® Corporation.
All rights reserved. No part of this book may be used or reproduced in any manner whatsoever without written permission from the publisher.
Printed in the United States of America. For information, contact
Perfection Learning® Corporation, 1000 North Second Avenue,
P.O. Box 500, Logan, Iowa 51546.
Paperback ISBN 0-7891-1963-3
Cover Craft® ISBN 07-807-6136-7

7 8 9 10 11 12 PP 10 09 08 07 06 05

Table of Contents

A Fun Place to Start

I tried to JAM this book full of fun and interesting stuff about pets.

You won't believe what you read in the first chapter! It's amazing what some owners do for their pets. Like pet collars with diamonds, photo sessions, and special boarding houses. And then there are the limo rides to the salon!

I hope you enjoy the funny chapters with pets talking to each other.

I also tried to answer some common questions about pets. Questions like "What pet is the *easiest* to care for?" and "How can you get a pet if you have little or no money?"

You'll read about all kinds of pets—from dogs to tree frogs. And yes, tree frogs can make good pets. But remember, it's best NOT TO DANCE with one.

Frogs are light on their feet. But people tend to fall out of trees!

PETS may chew up your shoes
And ruin your best chair,
But their love makes
Even a grouch
Less of a bear.

Anita Higman

Chapter 1

Caring to the MAX

What is "caring to the MAX"? It's checking your pet pig into a special boarding house for animals (with TV included). Or a bubble bath for your dog. With massaging water jets, no less. Followed, of course, by a doggy ice cream party for her and several of her best friends.

Sound strange? Believe it or not, some people do give their pets these special pampering treats. Would you like to do this for your pets? Well, come along with me for some interesting tales.

I spent some time talking with an animal lover named Suzanne. She owns a special boarding house for all kinds of pets. And she does some pretty special things for people's pets. She even won an award for her fine work with pets.

Question: What do you do for pets?

Answer: I take care of people's pets when they go out of town. But more and more, I'm taking care of pets on a daily basis. While their owners are at work. This is called doggy or kitty-cat day care.

Question: What are some of the special services you have for pets?

Answer:
1. We groom pets. It's important to keep their skin clean and healthy.
2. We give them birthday parties. With hats and special doggy cakes. And we send them birthday cards.
3. We also send get-well cards when pets are sick.
4. We have special holiday meals for pets.
5. We have a portable phone for pets to use. To talk to their owners who are away on trips.
6. Sometimes we use our pink van to take pets places. Like to the vet or to the airport to catch a flight.
7. If an owner is in the hospital, we take pictures of the pet.
8. Also, we have going-away parties for pets if they leave our area.

Fun Fact

Pigs eat snakes.

Question: What is a typical day like?

Answer: We have playtime, mealtime, TV time, a cookie break, and nap time. Plus, we have activities such as swimming and chasing and catching bubbles. We make sure all the pets have human contact. We say the pets' names over and over, because it reminds them of home. We show them love. And try to be their home away from home.
I feel stress can bring on illness. So, we do whatever we can to keep the pet stress-free.

Question: What are some of the unique places you have for the animals to stay?

Answer: We have special suites with TVs and ceiling fans. Our new building will have rooms with dinosaur, sports, and rock-and-roll themes. We're also putting in fake fireplaces.

Question: Do you take in all kinds of pets?

Answer: Yes. Rabbits, birds, reptiles, and fish are some of the animals that stay here. Pigs are also very popular pets that come here.

Question: What pets are becoming more popular?

Answer: We are seeing more and more birds as pets. Also more reptiles. But ferrets are not as popular as they used to be.

Question: What are some products that people like to buy for their pets?

Answer:
1. Toys that make noises
2. Toys that are stuffed with catnip (for cats)
3. Pet collars with diamonds on them
4. Cologne to mist on their fur
5. Doggy toothpaste
6. Nature videos (for relaxing)
7. Plush beds
8. Rain boots and coats
9. Hats with built-in sunglasses
10. Matching scarves for pets and their owners
11. Doggy cookies, bagels, and other goodies
12. Safe hair dyes to color their fur
13. Pet costumes for holiday dress-up

Fun Fact

Most blue-eyed cats are deaf.

Question: What should someone do if he loses his pet?

Answer: First, call your local vets and grooming shops. Ask them to put information on their bulletin boards. Hang plenty of signs in your neighborhood. And do it right away. Be specific on the sign. Offer a reward, if you can. Putting an article in your local newspaper should also help.

I met someone else who loves animals. Her name is Angel. She works in another very nice pet-care facility.

Angel and her employees also pamper people's pets. They even have a tiny two-room suite for cats. It has a fireplace, a round couch, and fluffy pillows. And, of course, there's a little lamp in the bedroom. Just enough light for someone to read kitty's favorite bedtime story.

Just like the other people I interviewed, Angel had lots of pets when she was growing up. Including a dog named Princess. And a pony named Birthday because she got him for her birthday.

Here is what Angel had to say about her fun job. And about taking care of pets.

Question: Besides basic care, what are some of the special things you offer pets?

Answer: Some owners sign up for special pet care. We'll do whatever that owner requests for his or her pet. Sometimes pets are scared when their owners leave. So we take them into the pet-care room. We let them sit on our laps with a blanket. Sometimes they just like their bellies rubbed. Or some extra hugs. Some pets come from other countries and are used to other languages. So we try to speak some comforting words in the language the animal is used to.

Question: What are some of the unique things you've seen people buy for their pets?

Answer:
1. Gift baskets made out of rawhide (the pets can eat them)
2. Lacy little dresses that make dogs look like Southern Belles
3. Doggy pajamas with little bears on them
4. A trip to the salon for nail polish and hair bows
5. Photo sessions or portrait sittings

Question: Do you have any pets?

Answer: Yes. I have dogs, a snake, and two horses. Our horses' names are Sassy and Sir. My husband and I enjoy taking our horses on the old-time trail rides.

Question: What are the basic items you will need before you bring your new dog home?

Answer:
1. Food and two bowls (for food and water)

2. Grooming equipment, like a good brush or comb (depending on the type of dog you get)
3. Healthy dog treats for rewards
4. A good leash and collar (for taking her to the vet and for walks)
5. A doghouse or some other type of shelter for outside dogs
6. A crate or indoor kennel for house dogs—or at least some type of bed area that's her very own

Fun Fact

The smallest horse in the world is the Fallabella. It is only 30 inches high. People housebreak these horses and keep them as pets.

7. Doggy toys, like a rawhide bone or a chewy rope toy (This will keep your pet occupied and out of trouble. She'll have something to chew on besides your shoes or the couch!)

Question: What is the best way to housebreak a puppy?

Answer: First, show your new puppy lots of attention. Put him on a schedule. Take him outside at certain times of the day. And when he goes to the bathroom outside, reward him. Make a big deal about it. Say, "What a good boy you are!"

Fun Fact

Cats are apparently color-blind. They see images only in shades of gray.

A safety crate or indoor kennel is the best place for your puppy to sleep. This will make him feel secure. Typically, dogs will not soil the place where they sleep. So it is best not to let your dog eat or drink while in the crate. And he shouldn't have a big bowl of water before bed.

If you do have to be away from the house, the crate will be a safe area for your puppy. And help keep him out of trouble.

Question: Should all dogs be walked daily?

Answer: All dogs don't *have* to be walked daily. But regular exercise and attention are healthy for your dog. You should spend about 10 to 15 minutes of good quality time with your pet each day. If you can't take him for a walk outside, scratch his belly. Or give him hugs.

Question: What do you need before you bring your new cat home?

Answer:	1. A kitty-litter box
	2. A scratching post (so she'll have something to scratch besides your furniture!)
	3. Food and two bowls (for food and water)
	4. A brush
	5. A little collar (Cats get special breakaway collars because they have a habit of jumping everywhere. So if the collar catches on something, it will break. And not cause your cat a problem.)
Question:	Why do you think kids need pets?
Answer:	Pets always understand and respond to you when you're happy. And if you get mad at them, they forgive you.
	Also, pets are good listeners. And they're always there to cheer you up. When I was a child and I was sad, my dog would snuggle with me.
Question:	Why do you work in the pet-care business?
Answer:	I love animals. So, this is a great job for me. My dream has always been to have a ranch and rescue animals. Like a homeless shelter for animals. And someday that dream will come true too.

Chapter 2

Six Great Cat Stories

Kids and adults can really grow to love their pets. And in their own ways, pets seem to love us back.

They don't care whether we have a lot of money. They don't care if we're famous or super smart. They just love us. I like that.

Cats are very popular pets. People never seem to tire of telling about their cats.

So I decided to dedicate a whole chapter just to cats. Below are six funny and odd stories about our feline friends and their owners.

The Amazing Journey

My father is a farmer. He was given a cat that he called Kitty Cat.

When Kitty Cat first arrived, she missed her old home. So one day she walked four long miles back to where she had lived.

Up and down the hills through the country she walked. And all the way back into town. Kitty Cat even found the right house.

It was amazing because Kitty Cat had only been on that road once. And she had been in a cage in a pickup. She couldn't even see the road. Animals are *truly amazing!*

My father got Kitty Cat back. And now she is happy on the farm. She has a new litter of kittens. And she has lots of attention from my father.

But my father has not forgotten Kitty Cat's amazing journey.

Kelsey and Barry are sister and brother. They've had a number of pets over the years. But none like their cat Crystal. Here are some true stories they told about Crystal and her pranks.

Fun Fact

Cats can move each ear separately.

The Cat Burglar

Our cat, Crystal, began making mischief early in life. Actually, when she was just a kitten.

One boring evening, she jumped from the kitchen table onto our birdcage. The cage began to swing wildly. The two birds inside were frantic.

As the birdcage swung higher, it slammed against the wall. All the banging startled my mom. She thought it was a burglar.

My mom crept downstairs. She didn't find a burglar. She found two scared birds and one scared kitty.

Crystal clung to the side of the cage. Crystal was just as scared as the birds. She wanted down!

The birds wished they had never met an animal called a cat. And my mom was just glad it was only a *pet* cat burglar.

Feline Frenzy

One day when we came home from school, Mom was worried. "I can't find Crystal anywhere," she said. "She's gone!"

So my father drove around the neighborhood to find her. He returned later with a cat. Dad also had lots of scratches.

The cat was *angry*. She jumped out of the car's sunroof. Then she ran under the garage door. It almost shut down on her tail. Then she raced back outside.

About this time, my mom came out. She was holding Crystal. "She was in the house the whole time," Mom said.

Suddenly, we understood why Dad's cat was so angry. And why she didn't want to be found.

One Hot Cat

Then there was the time Crystal decided to sample a spicy treat. We had been drying some red-hot peppers to season our food.

Crystal thought the red-hot peppers looked interesting. Usually, she didn't climb up on the kitchen counter. But her curiosity got the best of her.

We heard lots of noise and ran downstairs. Crystal's tail was straight up in the air. And her tongue was sticking out as she bounced around the room.

In her frenzy, she'd torn up a pile of white paper napkins. Bits of white had flown everywhere. It looked like a snowstorm in the living room.

Finally, Crystal cooled her mouth with some water from her bowl. And you know what? Crystal isn't curious about red-hot peppers anymore.

Fun Fact

Snakes smell with their tongues. A snake flicks its tongue out and gathers bits of odor. When its tongue goes back in its mouth, the odor particles transfer to a gland called Jacobson's Organ, which is in the roof of the mouth.

Remote Control Kitty

Once again in the middle of the night, Crystal was up to her mischief. She stepped onto the remote control button, turning on the TV.

The noise awakened my mom. "Who would be watching TV now?" she wondered.

The blaring TV spooked Crystal. Her eyes bugged out. And her hair puffed up. She looked like a giant fur ball.

Crystal had nearly scared herself right out of one of her nine lives! And yes, she limits her TV watching now.

My last story about cats comes from my husband. When he was growing up, he had a cat that thought he was a dog. They called him Kitteee.

Monster Cat

Kitteee was a monster of a cat. He had seven toes on each front paw. He weighed 21 heavy pounds and was covered with gobs of thick fur. He even had huge paws like a dog. And he thought he was a dog.

Kitteee jumped on us like a dog. He brought back a shoe if we threw it. He would sit on our laps like a dog and watch TV.

But Kitteee was still a cat. He loved cat food. And he never could get the hang of barking.

Chapter 3

Pet Peeves: If Pets Could Talk

What if pets could talk? Then they could tell us exactly what they want. And what we're doing wrong. That might be kind of helpful. It also might be kind of funny. Here's what they might say.

Two Dogs Talking

Ozzie: I sure wish my master would feed me something good. Hasn't he ever heard that real dogs don't eat cat food?

Paws: That's horrible. No dog should have to stomach that.

Ozzie: I know it. It's really bad. Lately I've been playing with balls of yarn. And the dog next door said I fetch like a cat.

Paws: That's it. You have to move out.

Ozzie: But I hate to go now.

Paws: Why?

Ozzie: Because my owner just bought me a new rubber mouse.

Two Chameleons Talking

Tut: I see you're new in the cage. A real green horn. Just listen up, kid. And you'll do okay here.

Our owners really like it when we change colors. So do lots of that. Oh, and they like to see us watching two things at once. They nearly bust a gut laughing when they see our eyes moving around separately. And when you're catching bugs, stretch your tongue out as far as you can. It gives them the creeps. But they love it.

Well, that about covers it. Do you have any questions?

Dinky: Yeah. What *don't* we do?

Tut: Well, the other day, our owners put a big purple ball in the cage to get me to change color. I nearly exploded trying to make myself blend in. So, *that's* where we draw the line. We're not going to do *purple!*

Two Parrots Talking

Wing: You know, for a parrot, you sure don't say much.

Echo: Well, I'm just not a blabber-beak gossip like you.

Wing: That hurts my feelings. Say you're sorry.

Echo: Oh, don't get your feathers so ruffled. Besides, my owner never taught me how to say I'm sorry.

Wing: That remark just doesn't fly.

Echo: Neither do I. My wings are clipped.

Wing: So, what *can* you say?

Echo: Nothing. My owner never talks to me. I've decided I'm not going to be a "talker" anyway.

Wing: Well, you're talking *now,* aren't you?

Echo: Yes. But I'll never repeat a word of it.

Fun Fact

The kea parrot of New Zealand hunts and eats sheep.

Two Gerbils Talking

Paddy: What happened to you? You look awful.

Lulu: Well, my master gave me all the wrong food. I got too big. So then he decided I needed to lose weight. He put a motor on my exercise wheel. I've been running for hours. I thought I'd never get off that crazy wheel.

Paddy: How awful!

Lulu: I got him back, though.

Paddy: How?

Lulu: I got out of my cage. Then I did my best rat imitation the last time his lady friend was over. I don't think she'll be spending too much time around here anymore!

Two Snakes Talking

Rip: I'm really angry. Do you want to know why? Well, I'll tell you. I'm tired of being called the *other* "s" word. I'm not slimy. I've never been slimy. I wash every day. I use deodorant. I use mouthwash. So even my mouth isn't slimy. I'm dry. Get it? And if somebody calls me *slimy* one more time, I'll come *unglued!*

Keely: Is that why we shed our skin? I always wondered about that.

Two Fish Talking

Fin: Have I ever told you that you're special?

Flora: Not really. And I sure don't feel very special.

Fin: Well, you should. Sure, I know there are about 40,000 different kinds of us in the world. But you and I are still very special.

Flora: Why?

Fin: Because we are sloshing around in this bag together.

Flora: So? What does that have to do with anything?

Fin: It means we've been chosen to be somebody's pet. We're going home with someone. They'll have a special little water home just for us. No more plain store tank!

Flora: I just hope our owner knows how to feed us. And take care of us. Do you think he remembered to pick up a booklet about us at the pet store? What if the tank isn't big enough? What if he puts us in with big fish? They could eat us for lunch. A lot could go wrong here!

Fin: You worry too much. By the way, what is that giant thing looking at us?

Flora: I think it's our owner's nose pressed up against our bag.

Fin: Wow! Was that an earthquake?

Flora: I think someone dropped us. Oh no. Now he's poking the bag to see if we're still alive. Quick! Swim around. Then he'll leave us alone.

Fin: You know, I liked the tank at the store. And I miss the other fish. Hey! We've changed our minds! Hey, you up there. Take us back to the store. HELP!

Two Pot-bellied Pigs Talking

Ping: My stomach hurts.

Pong: I'm not surprised. I saw what you had for breakfast. Two bananas, some toast crusts, milk, apple peelings, leftover Jell-O, and two doughnut holes. You eat like a garbage disposal!

Ping: That's not why my stomach hurts. I got a splinter in it last night. It's painful having your stomach drag on the floor.

Pong: Why do you think they call us pot-bellied pigs?

Ping: I've seen pictures of other pigs. They're lean and sleek. Their bellies don't sag.

Pong: Be glad your stomach does sag. Those other pigs are packages of bacon by now. I don't think a slice of you would fit on a sandwich.

Ping: I still wish my stomach was firmer. Maybe I should do some exercises.

Pong: Look, just be glad humans think we're cute. We have a better life than most pigs.

Ping: We deserve it. We're quieter than dogs. We're smarter than cats.

Pong: We are?

Ping: Sure we are. Did you see Fluff chasing that bird yesterday? That bird wasn't big enough for a snack! You'd never catch me chasing something like that.

Pong: Yeah, but you'd chase a barrel of chicken if it was rolling down the street.

Ping: That's different. Chicken is hoof-licking good!

Pong: We don't have hooves, silly. We have feet.

Ping: Okay, then. Chicken is feet-licking good.

Pong: That's disgusting. Shhh! Here comes our human now. Stand still and look cute!

Ping: I just wish she'd quit calling me Wilbur.

Chapter 4

Got a Pet Question? Let's Ask a Vet

I found a great pet doctor named Dr. Duncan. I asked him all kinds of questions about pets.

Dr. Duncan grew up on a ranch in Texas. He was always around animals. And he had lots of pets.

As early as third grade, he knew he wanted to be a vet. And you can tell. He still loves what he does.

Dr. Duncan now has two dogs. Their names are Magnum and Penny. He also has a cat named Clifford.

Here is what Dr. Duncan had to say about pets.

Question: What pets did you have as a boy?

Answer: We had dogs and cats. And I had all kinds of wild pets too. I had pet raccoons, coyotes, deer, bobcats, and peccaries. But I don't think keeping wild pets is a good idea anymore because of rabies.

Question: What is a peccary?

Answer: It's like a pig.

Question: Is it true that pigs make good pets?

Answer: Yes. And they are very intelligent too.

Question: What pets do you enjoy now?

Answer: Mostly dogs. But I enjoy working with all animals. And I like the exotic pets too.

Question: What are the best pets for kids?

Answer: Dogs and cats make good pets. But if you don't have room for them, try the small pets. Like mice and hamsters and gerbils.

Question: So, you don't think wild animals make good pets?

Answer: No. As I said, I do not recommend that at all. I had them when I was a kid. But most of the time, you can't tame them. And they can be dangerous. And there is always the threat of getting rabies.

Fun Fact

Some lizards can run up to 18 miles per hour.

Question: Is it all right to pet a stray cat, dog, or other animal?

Answer: No. You should never approach any animal that you don't know.

Question: Should pets have shots?

Answer: Yes, most of them. Check with your vet for the shots your pet needs.

Question: What pet is the easiest to care for?

Answer: Probably some of the exotics. Like hermit crabs or a skink.

Question: What is a skink?

Answer: It is a type of lizard.

Question: How can you get a pet if you have little or no money?

Answer: You can adopt dogs and cats from a shelter. Or when someone in the neighborhood has a litter of kittens or pups they're giving away. But remember, caring for a pet costs money.

Question: What is the most expensive pet to own?

Answer: Probably a horse. You have to have a lot of equipment. It costs more to feed them. And you have to have a place to keep them.

Question: Do you think a pet and its owner can really understand each other?

Answer: Yes, to a certain extent.

Question: One of our neighbors is really mean to his dog. He kicks him and doesn't feed him most of the time. Is that against the law?

Answer: Yes. Nearly everywhere there are laws against animal abuse. If you see animal abuse, you should tell an adult.

Fun Fact

A pig can live as long as 27 years.

Fun Fact

Foals (baby horses) are born with their eyes open.

Question: How is it that parrots sound like people?

Answer: They can mimic the voices of people. Certain types of parrots are better than others at doing this.

Question: How do you get a parrot to start talking?

Answer: Just repeat phrases over and over.

Question: What are the best kinds of birds for kids to own?

Answer: A parakeet or some of the other small birds, like canaries or finches. They are easier to care for.

Question: How should I care for my pet bird?

Answer: You should be very careful about his diet.

Question: How does a new owner know what a proper diet is?

Answer: Pick up a brochure at the pet store. If you're still unsure, ask your vet. Some vets specialize in caring for birds. They are called *avian vets.*

Question: My dog won't stop barking. How can I get him to stop?

Answer: It depends on why the dog is barking. If there's somebody in the neighborhood aggravating him, that's one thing. If he just sits out in the backyard and barks because nobody's out there with him, that's another. If you have a dog that's a problem barker, call your vet. Explain what the dog is doing. Once you know why the dog is barking, the vet can help you.

Question: My dog has fleas and ticks. How can I get rid of them?

Answer: There are lots of ways to handle that. Contact your vet. She'll tell you which types of products are safe to use.

Question: Do other animals get fleas and ticks?

Answer: Yes. Most of your warm-blooded animals can get both fleas and ticks. Cold-blooded animals, like snakes and lizards, just get ticks.

Question: Sometimes my dog likes to eat what I'm eating. Is that okay?

Answer: No. You should never get dogs started on table foods. They need to be on a balanced diet. Consult your vet. Even some of the dog foods are not that good.

Question: My dog's hair is really matted. Should I do anything about it?

Answer: Comb out the mats, if you can. Otherwise, clip them off. If they're thick mats, you might have to shave them off.

Question: Why is matting a problem?

Answer: Because dogs can get skin infections.

Question: What can I do about my dog's bad breath?

Answer: You can brush his teeth. If it's really bad, take him to your vet. The vet will check his teeth. Some of them may be decayed. Your dog may need to have his teeth cleaned. Then you can begin to brush them.

Question: Do vets do dental work?

Answer: Yes. Some do. And there are some vets that do dental work only.

Question: Do snakes and lizards make good pets?

Answer: *Some* do. They can be pretty easy to care for, if you start them out right. Find out *everything* you need to know about them *first*.

Fun Fact

A dog's wet nose helps it sniff out odors. There is a gland in a dog's nose that helps it stay wet. If the nose does dry out, a dog will lick it to keep it moist.

Question: What kind of pet snake would you recommend?

Answer: A corn snake. Start with a docile one. Buy it from a reputable breeder or pet store. And check the diet requirements first.

Question: Why don't my dog and cat get along?

Answer: It's probably because they weren't raised with each other. Or maybe the dog was raised to chase cats. Or the cat might be naturally afraid of dogs. With time and your training, though, they might learn to get along.

Question: I want to buy a rabbit. What do I need?

Answer: You'll need a rabbit hutch or cage. Then you'll need to read a booklet on proper care. Your vet can help you too. A rabbit's diet is very important. For example, lettuce has almost no nutritional benefit to the rabbit.

Question: How big does my rabbit cage have to be?

Answer: It depends on the type and weight of the rabbit.

Question: Do rabbits get lonely? Will I need to buy two of them?

Answer: No. They're like dogs and cats. They get along well by themselves.

Question: Do rabbits need exercise?

Answer: Yes. Let the rabbit out of his cage to exercise. Be careful that your grass hasn't been sprayed with any type of poison.

Fun Fact

Rabbits cannot walk or run. They can only hop.

Question: My cat is tearing up my bedroom furniture. How can I get her to stop?

Answer: There are many things you can do. There's now a product to help. They're like soft covers to glue over claws. But they have to be replaced. Or some people have their cat's front paws declawed. Sometimes a scratching post helps. When you see your cat on the furniture, take her to the scratching post. And let her know she's not supposed to scratch the furniture.

Question: Does my cat need regular checkups?

Answer: Yes. Once a year.

Question: Do *all* pets need checkups?

Answer: Most do. Check with your vet about your pet. It's important for most pets to get an annual checkup. Sometimes a semiannual checkup is necessary when the pets get older. Also, as soon as you get a new pet, you should take her to a vet for a checkup.

Question: What is catnip? Can I give some to my cat?

Answer: It's an herb. Give it to your cat. Most cats love it!

Question: Where can I get it?

Answer: You can buy it at pet shops. Sprinkle it on one of your cat's toys or his bedding. Cats like to roll in it and smell it and lick it.

Question: My cat is about to have kittens. Should I do something extra for her?

Answer: Once again, make sure she's on a good diet. If you have any doubts, call your vet to make sure everything is proper for her.

Question: My cat is really overweight. Does he need a special diet?

Answer: Yes. If he's overweight, give him less food. Or try to increase his exercise. You may need to change to a special low-calorie cat food.

Question: I just got a kitten. How am I supposed to teach her about the litter box?

Answer: Most of the time, it's a natural instinct. Put your new kitten in the litter box. She'll figure it out right away. Clean the litter box at least every other day. Then you shouldn't have any accidents.

Question: I have a female cat. Am I supposed to get her spayed?

Answer: Yes, unless she's registered and you plan to sell the kittens. Or you plan to raise the kittens or know someone who will. Cats make better pets when they're spayed. (This is true for dogs also.) It's important not to add to the population of unwanted animals.

Question: Do you ever doctor pet fish?

Answer: Yes. All sizes.

Question: How?

Answer: Most of the time, I treat the water.

Question: What's the most unusual pet you've ever doctored?

Answer: I suppose a moray eel.

Question: What is a moray eel?

Answer: It's a brightly colored eel with sharp teeth. They live in warm seas.

Question: What would you tell kids before they get a pet?

Answer: Pets are a big responsibility. They are entirely dependent upon you. You have to make sure they have food and water and shelter. And they need lots of attention. They need to be with someone. They want to be talked to. They want to be loved and petted. If you want an animal, you should be willing to do these things.

Question: Do all animals need that same kind of affection?

Answer: Yes. Even lizards seem to respond to it.

Question: Is there anything else you'd like to add?

Answer: Remember to give your pet proper nutrition and love. I guess those are the two most important things.

Fun Fact

The glass lizard sheds its tail if it is attacked. The tail keeps on wiggling even after it comes off. The other animal chases the wiggling tail, and the lizard escapes. Its tail grows back in a few days.

Chapter 5

Three Super Short Stories

I grew up on a farm in Oklahoma. I loved pets. And I had a lot of them! At different times, I had a pet turtle, frog, snake, chicken, rooster, pig, rabbit, dog, and many cats. Here are three of my true pet stories.

Fun Fact

Asian glider snakes can parachute from tall trees to the ground. As they fall, they spread their ribs. This helps their bodies catch the air and slows their fall.

Herby Flake, My Pet Snake

Believe it or not, one of my favorite pets was my snake. I named him Herby Flake. I chose "Flake" so that his name would rhyme with *snake*. In case I wanted to write songs about him.

Anyway, Herby was easy to get along with. And he was fun to be with. Even my mother didn't mind him too much. As long as I didn't play with him in the kitchen!

I had to leave Herby behind when I went to college. There were no Herbies allowed.

My Baby Pig

We raised a lot of hogs on our farm. One time, one of the newborn pigs became ill. I asked my father if I could doctor him. And then keep him as my pet. My dad said yes.

I just knew a pig would make a great pet. And I thought I could make him well.

Sadly, he didn't live very long. It was not a happy time.

But sometimes pets die. That's the bad part of owning and loving pets.

18 Cats!

Cats were always a favorite of mine. I remember that we had 18 cats on our farm at one time.

Now I know we probably shouldn't have had so many cats. We let our feline population get way out of hand.

But I did love cats. And I had plenty to love.

Our cats loved to eat. Even brown bugs. You know, the kind that buzz at the porch light on a summer night. Anyway, our cats used to love to eat them. I never knew whether it was the flavor or the crunchy texture that they liked.

I also remember dressing up my kittens. I'd get them all fancied up. I'd push them in my doll buggy. I pretended they were real babies.

But thinking back, that probably wasn't too fair. I suppose cats need their space too. Just like people.

Chapter 6

Unusual Pets

This time I talked to a rancher. Her name is Christine. She is a breeder of some unusual pets. She has pot-bellied pigs, chinchillas, doves, Angora bunnies, and ducks.

Christine told me about the joys of raising and caring for these animals. These pets may not be quite right for your backyard or home, but they are still fun to learn about!

Question: What can you tell us about pot-bellied pigs?

Answer: Pot-bellied pigs are very smart. (So are pigs in general.) They stay very small. They can be house-trained like a dog. And even do tricks like a dog. They take a special feed (pot-bellied pig pellets). You need to be careful not to overfeed them. It's best not to add to their diet. Treats are okay, though, if you're teaching them to do tricks. Grapes and apple slices are good.

Even though regular pigs are clean, there is a body odor to them. But pot-bellied pigs don't have an odor like a regular pig.

One of my pot-bellied pigs is named Maggie. She does tricks. She can play dead. Then she'll roll over for you to scratch her belly.

Question: So pot-bellied pigs are good pets?

Answer: Yes. They're tame and gentle. If they're handled right. Like any animal, they need to be treated kindly. You should start with them when they're a baby. I would suggest a female over a male. Unless the male has his tusks removed and he's neutered.

Question: What are some basic care items for a pot-bellied pig?

Answer: They need fresh water at all times. That's important for any animal. And they need that special food I mentioned. I feed mine once a day instead of twice a day. They also need a clean pen with a shelter.

Question: Do chinchillas make good pets?

Answer: Under supervision, this animal would do all right as a pet. Since chinchillas are nocturnal, they are up at night. So a kid's room might not be the best place for them.
They are somewhat like a hamster or gerbil. But bigger. You have to be very careful about the way you pick them up. They should be picked up at the base of the tail.
If you started chinchillas young enough, they would be a pet you could cuddle and hold. But you would need to be careful. Because chinchillas do like to gnaw on things. And that could be your finger!

Question: What kind of doves do you have?

Answer: I have ring-necked doves. I feed them birdseed. And fresh water. Their cages are cleaned on a regular basis. I hang wicker baskets cut in half from the tops of their cages. So they can nest.

Question: Do you think ring-necked doves make good pets?

Answer: Yes, I do.

Question: What is something you really like about your doves?

Answer: I like to talk to them with little cooing noises. And they coo back to me. It's a very relaxing, peaceful sound.

Question: Would you recommend an Angora bunny for a pet?

Answer: Well, Angora rabbits are a lot of work. They need a lot of grooming. This pet would be better for someone who has a lot of time. Do keep in mind that rabbits are like rodents. They like to gnaw on things. Even your finger. But Angora bunnies are beautiful animals with their long hair. Mine are light brown. And they are *so soft* and cuddly.

Question: What do you feed your Angora rabbits?

Answer: I give them fresh water and a good rabbit pellet. As a special treat, I sometimes give them vegetables and hay.

Question: What about ducks as pets?

Answer: Well, ducks aren't very cuddly pets. But they are fun to watch. So you could "adopt" some ducks that live in a nearby pond. When you take food to them, they will come up to you. And it seems like they're talking.

I have a pet duck named Mamma Duck. She likes to waddle behind me. And follow me *everywhere*.

Question: What is your favorite animal?

Answer: I couldn't choose. I enjoy each one in a different way.

Fun Fact

Female rabbits can have new litters five times in a year. Baby rabbits are called *kittens*.

Chapter 7

More Pet Peeves: If Pets Could Talk

I hope you enjoyed the talking animals in Chapter 3. Below are some more wacky pets telling us how it is.

Two Rabbits Talking

Bun: Did you hear that awful growl? I think they're coming.

Rab: Who's coming?

Bun: You know. Those big hairy things that bark.

Rab: You mean dogs? They scare the hoppers out of me.

Bun: I'm afraid they'll chew me up. And then use me for pillow stuffing. The ones on two legs without the bark aren't much better.

Rab: You mean humans?

Bun: How would they feel if we picked them up by their ears? What do they think we are? Suitcases? EARS ARE NOT HANDLES!

Rab: Yeah, that really hurts.

> ### Fun Fact
>
> Rabbits hop up to 18 miles per hour. That's faster than people can run!

Bun: In fact, I think it's making my ears sag. Do you think I look lop-eared?

Rab: Now let's not "jump" to conclusions. I just wish they'd clean my cage. My food smells like last week's garbage.

Bun: Do you know what else? I heard one of the humans call my baby hairless and ugly.

Rab: Now that's going a "hare" too far. Imagine them calling us hairless! Look at all that hairless, pink skin they have. They need some fur.

Bun: Yeah, that bare skin is really ugly. I guess that's why some of them take our fur and wear it!

Rab: I thought that was an old rabbit's tale.

Bun: I wish. I heard another growl.

Rab: Yeah, it's my stomach this time. I'm pretty hungry.

Bun: Me too. I hope we get fed today. My stomach is getting *so* small and my ears are getting *so* big. Pretty soon, I'll look like a mouse with elephant ears!

Two Chameleons Talking

Camilla: Carl? Carl? Are you in here?

Carl: I'm over here in the corner.

Camilla: You look like a sandpile.

Carl: Of course I do. I'm sitting on a sandpile! I'm trying to rest. I had a terrible morning.

Camilla: Why?

Carl: Our human put me on a plaid couch! We chameleons are really good at changing colors. But have you ever tried to turn plaid?

Camilla: You think that's bad. I had to spend yesterday afternoon on a flowered bedspread. I couldn't turn into a tulip! And I tried!

Carl: I'd rather be flowered than plaid. I felt like a pair of golf pants!

Camilla: Speaking of golf, I wish we could go outside on the grass. I'd really like to snack on some nice, fresh grass. I get tired of this Purina Lizard Chow he feeds us.

Carl: I know. It's silly. The humans use machines to cut the grass, but we would be happy to do it for them.

Camilla: You bet. Still, it's nice in here.

Carl: That's true. There are lots of branches to climb on. We have a nice flat rock to sit on. Our humans give us plenty of clean water. Best of all, there is the lovely sun that shines right over our home.

Camilla: What sun?

Carl: You know. The one with "GE" printed on it.

Camilla:	That's a lightbulb, you loopy lizard. The humans put it there to keep us warm.
Carl:	Well, it's nice anyway.
Camilla:	Look! What's that?
Carl:	Where?
Camilla:	Behind you! Stick out your eyes and take a look!
Carl:	Gee, I'm glad my eyes can see two ways at once. It saves a lot of wear and tear on my neck.
Camilla:	Never mind your neck. What is that creature?
Carl:	Oh, it's just a cat.
Camilla:	A cat!
Carl:	A cat!
Camilla:	Can I join you on that sandpile?
Carl:	Be my guest. We'll fade into the background until that cat leaves.

Two Cats Talking

Catlin:	Wow! Is that some kind of new fur-do?
Faline:	Isn't it awful? It's sticking straight up. It looks like I got shocked.
Catlin:	Well, what do you expect? Your owner treats you like a toy.
Faline:	It's scary. Every day he finds some new torture for me. Last week, he jammed me into a plastic car. And sent me flying down a steep hill. Yesterday, he shoved me out on a toy sailboat into the middle of a pond.
Catlin:	What did you do?
Faline:	I did what *any* self-respecting cat would do. I pretended not to care. Then he had to come and get

Fun Fact

Mice eat almost anything, including glue and soap.

me. He got soaking wet. I tried not to laugh, but it was hard.

But I still have a few tricks up my fur. Tonight, I'm coughing up some fur balls to put in his shoes. And tomorrow, I'm planning to present him with a little surprise on his breakfast plate.

Catlin: What's that?

Faline: A dead mouse. I've been saving it for a *very* long time.

Two Ducks Talking

Lotty: What do you know, Grace?

Grace: Not a thing, Lotty.

Lotty: Well, I heard through the barnyard that Meg Mallard is going to tell that cat what she thinks of him. Someone has to do it. That cat is always up to no good. Especially when it comes to us helpless ducks. Anyway, this is the big day.

Grace: Do tell.

Lotty: Meg is going to waddle right up to that cat and spit in her furry little stuck-up face.

Grace: Can ducks spit?

Lotty: She can *now*. The dog has been teaching her.

Grace: You don't mean that Meg Mallard is friends with the dog. No way!

Lotty: It's true. The whole barnyard is talking about it. A dog and a duck. Friends.

Anyway, the dog has had it with the cat too. Last week, the dog tried to take a nap under the pecan tree. Well, the cat shook the tree and opened fire on him. About a million of those nuts hit him on the head. He says he's still a little dizzy-headed from the whole thing.

Grace: Well, if you ask me, the dog has always been a little funny in the head.

Lotty: I know just what you mean. In fact, Meg's a little fuzzy-brained too.

Grace: Whatever do you mean?

Lotty: Well, for one thing, Meg never swims with the rest of us.

Grace: You're right.

Lotty: And as if that's not weird enough. Now she's dropping her eggs everywhere. She even laid one in the pond!

Grace: NO!

Lotty: Yes! I'm afraid so. Ghastly business. And no one knows about it but me. Can you just imagine what a dreadful strain it was for me to keep such a secret?

Grace: You feel better now that you've told me, don't you?

Lotty: Well, not really. Because I've actually told about twenty other friends. But still, no one's supposed to know. So the secret is still my burden to bear. Do you know what I mean?

Grace: Yes. I can imagine how you've suffered. So tell me, what happens to Meg when the farmer finds out she's laying her eggs in the pond?

Lotty: Well, Meg's best friend claims it's all the farmer's fault. He should pen her up at night like the rest of us.

Grace: Well, she is the farmer's pet, don't you know?

Lotty: Yes, and she knows it too. The way she holds her head just a little too high.

So are you going to watch Meg give it to the cat? I heard they're setting up seats on the waterfront. And they're going to sell bags of grain for the show.

Grace: Oh, I don't know. It's going to be such a silly spectacle.

Lotty: Well, it should be scads of fun to watch.

Grace: Why?

Lotty: Because I heard the cat is armed and ready with a sack of pecans.

Grace: Well, like I said. Save a place for me!

Two Turtles Talking

Racer: Are *you* thinking what *I'm* thinking?

Shelly: I don't know. I'm so bored. I can't remember *how* to think.

Racer: Well, I was thinking how great it was to live outside. Trees, ponds, sunshine, and all the worms we could eat.

Shelly: Now we're stuck in this tiny glass box with nothing to do. No rocks to climb. No flowers to pick. No bugs to scare. *Boring!*

Racer: It's freezing in here too. And I haven't been feeling well since somebody painted my shell.

Shelly: Hey, maybe we could bust out of this joint.

Racer: How?

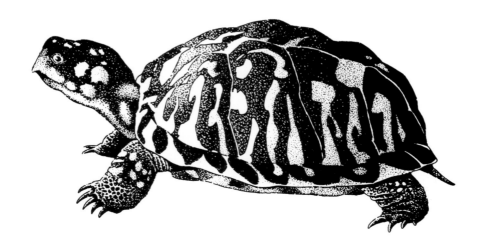

Shelly: Well, the next time that big creature with the funny face picks us up, we'll snap his nose. Then we'll make our getaway.

Racer: The last time I tried that, he dropped me. That fall nearly broke my shell. And you know what *that* means.

Shelly: Yeah—the big turtle graveyard.

Racer: If there's no way out, then we'll just have to go on a food strike.

Shelly: No! Not that! You know how I love those sweet, gooey slugs.

Racer: Then we'll have to stop being so social.

Shelly: That's it. The perfect idea. We'll just close up our gates and hibernate!

Two Tadpoles Talking

Tad: So, what kind of tadpole are you?

Polly: A land toad.

Fun Fact

Frogs shed their skin many times a year. Then they usually eat the old skin.

Tad: Oh, yeah? So am I. Why do you look different?

Polly: I guess I'm a different kind of toad. But we can still be friends.

Tad: I'm not so sure. You *are* munching on *my* algae. And you're in *my* personal space.

Polly: That's because we're getting too big for this tank. Haven't you noticed? We have our lungs and legs now. If we don't find a way out, will we drown?

Tad: Beats me. But I'm not hanging around here to find out.

Polly: What will we do?

Tad: We? Hey, buddy, it's each toad for himself.

Polly: Maybe we could help each other out of the tank.

Tad: But we're two different toads.

Polly: So what? We're still toads. And if we don't help each other out, we might be two *dead toads!*

Tad: Good point. Need a leg up?

Two Goats Talking

Billy: What is that thing in my hay?

Nanny: Maybe it's a piece of the sun.

Billy: Are you crazy? That's impossible. It could be a shooting star.

Nanny: If it is, I guess it stopped shooting.

Billy: It looks dead, whatever it is.

Nanny: I don't think the farmer would put anything dead in our hay.

Billy: Why don't you try tasting it?

Nanny: Because it looks sharp. We could try sniffing it.

Billy: Sure. Good idea. Go ahead.

Nanny: I can't. I have a cold. My sinuses have been clogged all day. Why don't *you* sniff it?

Billy: Maybe it's not something to sniff. Maybe it's just something to talk about.

Nanny:	I think you're afraid of it.
Billy:	Me? Afraid of a little shiny thing in my hay? Never.
Nanny:	Then try it.
Billy:	Try what?
Nanny:	The shiny thing.
Billy:	I'm just not in the mood.
Nanny:	Maybe we could just turn it over. Then we might be able to tell what it is.
Billy:	I thought of that already.
Nanny:	Why didn't you do it?
Billy:	Because there's writing on the other side. And goats don't read.
Nanny:	Oh. Yeah, that's right. Well, let's look anyway.
Billy:	Hey, that's a picture of people food on the front. And you know what people food comes in.
Nanny:	I can't believe it. It's a *tin can!*
Billy:	You're right. That's it.
Nanny:	How could the farmer be so … human? Did he really think that we'd eat a *tin can?* How barbaric!
Billy:	I hope he doesn't expect us to eat tin cans. I'm not giving up my grain. And if I don't get grain, he can just forget about me pulling his cart.
Nanny:	And I'll stop giving that creamy milk he loves so much.
Billy:	But then again, maybe the breeze tumbled the tin can into our hay by mistake.
Nanny:	The March wind does that sometimes. Come to think of it, last year I think the same thing happened. So I guess there's no need for us to be upset.
Billy:	No. I guess not. Wait. What's that shiny thing next to the barn?!

Chapter 8

Twenty-five Smart Pet Tips

1. Remember, almost all pets have the potential to bite.
2. Because of germs, it's important to wash your hands after you clean your pet's cage. Also, wash your hands after handling your pet.
3. Before you buy a pet, check to make sure no one in your family has allergies to pet dander.
4. Make sure you have a care plan before you buy a pet. Decide who will feed, water, and take care of the pet daily. Make sure you have all the equipment and food you need.
5. Plan carefully before you buy an exotic or unusual pet. Keep in mind that it might be too hard for a young person to care for.
6. Check with your vet to see if your pet should be spayed or neutered. Then get it done *before* you have a houseful of baby animals.
7. Make sure you'll still have room for the pet when he's full grown.

8. Don't abandon an unwanted pet. Call your local animal shelter. The people there will help you find another home for your pet.

9. Wild animals do *not* make good pets.

10. Be kind to your pets. A dog that is kicked or a cat that is squeezed too hard (even out of love) may become an angry animal. A gentle pet may bite if he or she is treated cruelly.

11. Some pets may be all right for older kids, but *not* for a younger brother or baby sister. It might be a good idea to ask your vet about the best pets for *your* household.

12. Check with your vet about preventing your pet from getting diseases. Some, like rabies, can be transmitted to humans. And ask how to prevent the passing of fungi and parasites from your animal to you and your family.

13. Put some sort of I.D. (identification) tag on your dog and cat. This will help if your pet gets lost.

14. Remember, having a pet means commitment. Dogs can live up to 15 years. Cats can live even longer. Are you willing to care for this pet for its lifetime?

15. You may want to consider obedience training for your dog. Or at least read a good book on the subject. It will help you and your dog get along better.

16. Pets should *never* be used to baby-sit a child.

17. Check with your local authorities before you decide on a pet. Make sure the pet you've chosen complies with all the laws.

18. Learn about *rabies*. Check out a book on this topic at your local library.

19. Dogs and cats, in some areas, need licenses. If your pet gets lost, the license will help you find her.

20. Consider adopting a pet from a local shelter.

21. Think of your pet when you travel. Take care of everything ahead of time. If you're flying, call your airline. Ask about their specific requirements for your pet.
22. Do not allow your pets to run loose in your neighborhood.
23. If your area is going to have bad weather, please remember the needs of your pet.
24. Make sure your pet has a comfortable place to sleep.
25. Set aside a special day for your pet. Spend some extra time together.

A Great Place to End

There are *so many* pets to choose from. I hope you have enjoyed learning about some of them. If you want to know about a special breed of dog or type of pet snake, check with your library.

I bet you thought I'd forgotten about tree frogs. No way. As I said in the beginning, tree frogs can make good pets. Some are very hardy. And they're fun to watch.

You can put tree frogs in a vivarium. It's like an aquarium. But it's set up with part land and part water.

Tree frogs eat live crickets and other bugs. You can buy live crickets at most pet stores.

Before buying tree frogs, read *all* the information you can about them *first*. Get all set up with the right equipment. And then enjoy.

If you do choose to have a pet, I wish you the very best in your search for the right one for you and your family. And I hope you have many years of fun and companionship with your special pet.